Hinduism For Kids: Beliefs And Practices

By

Shalu Sharma

ISBN-13: 978-1495370427
ISBN-10: 1495370429
Publisher: CreateSpace Independent Publishing Platform, North Charleston, SC

Table of contents

What is Hinduism?

Hinduism is an ancient religion. It is a collection of many thoughts, beliefs and rituals connected with preserving mother earth and the cycles of nature.

It originated in the Indian subcontinent before 2000 B.C. The main concepts in Hinduism are **Dharma** (duty), **Karma** (action), **Aatma** (soul), **Varna** (caste), **Guru** (teacher), and **Rebirth**.

Many Gods and Goddesses are worshipped in Hinduism, among whom Vishnu, Shiva, Brahma, Parvati, Lakshmi, Ganesha and Saraswati are the main ones.

The holy books of Hinduism are the Vedas, the Samhitas, the Upanishads, Bhagavad Gita, and the Ramayana. Hindus celebrate many festivals such as Diwali (festival of lights), Navaratri (worship of Goddess Durga), and Holi (festival of colours).

Who are the Hindus?

Hindus are those who accept and follow the religious, traditional and philosophical rules and regulations of Hinduism. Originally, the word 'Hindu' was meant to describe all those who live in Hindustan (India).

The word **'Hindustan'** refers to the "land of the Indus River" which is actually the Indian subcontinent. A Hindu is expected to perform the primary duties of life and follow the way of life that is mentioned in the Vedic scriptures. Many tribes and communities in India have contributed to the formation of the Hindu culture.

In India, there are many temples where different Gods and Goddesses are worshipped, some of which are the Jagannath Temple in Orissa, the Sripuram Golden Temple in Tamil Nadu, Akshardham in Delhi, and the Kashi Vishwanath Temple in Uttar Pradesh and so on.

Where do Hindus live?

Hindus are primarily **residents of India**. It is estimated that out of 100 Hindus in the world, more than 90 are from India. The growth of the Hindu religion began in India but the religion spread to different parts of the world many centuries ago. Neighboring countries such as Pakistan, Sri Lanka and Bangladesh also have small populations of Hindus. Before democracy came to Nepal, it was the world's only country with Hinduism as the official religion.

Countries of the Far East with Hindus include Indonesia, Malaysia, Cambodia and Thailand. The world's largest Hindu temple is in Angkor, a place in Cambodia. Many Hindus also live in the US and UK among other places in the world.

Where do Hindus worship?

Hindus worship in temples. In Sanskrit, temple is called '**Mandir**'. A Mandir is a structure in which the deity is housed. In the olden days, temples were made of stone or wood. Modern temples are made of concrete and also of stone.

Traditionally, temples were not only a place of worship; they were also places of cultural gatherings. All villages in India have a temple and it would be the site where teachers would hold classes on religious matters, village elders would discus important matters to do with the village, everyone would gather on important festivals and so on.

Temples can be tiny and set by the roadside, or they can be huge with magnificent decorations. North Indian temple style is different from South Indian temple style.

When was Hinduism discovered?

Hinduism grew over time and is one of the most ancient religions of the world. Experts differ as to the exact time it originated. But it is thought to have begun in the period between 1500 to 500 B.C.

Unlike other major world religions, Hinduism did not begin as an invention by a single person. It developed over time in the culture of Hindustan, the present name of India. As it grew bit by bit, powerful sages and groups began controlling the way it would develop.

The Vedas which are the basic holy books of the Hindus came to be written. These contain the primary rules and regulations of traditional Hinduism.

What are the Hindu holy books?

The Hindus have various holy books such as the Vedas, the Upanishads, and the two epics called the Ramayana and the Mahabharata, and the Puranas. In the beginning, these books were oral stories told by the ancient people that were passed on to one generation to another. Gradually, they were put down in written form to make the holy books of the Hindus.

The Vedas are the oldest of the Hindu holy books. The four most important Vedas are the Rig Veda, Atharva Veda, Yajur Veda and Sama Veda. The **Bhagavad Gita**, an off-shoot of the Mahabharata, is also an important holy Hindu book containing the teachings of Lord Krishna.

The sacred texts are all written in Sanskrit.

What are the Vedas?

The Vedas are the holy books of the Hindus containing a depth of spiritual and philosophical meaning. Veda in Sanskrit means **'knowledge'**. There are 4 Vedas: the Yajur Veda, the Atharva Veda, Sama Veda and the Rig Veda. They are all written in Vedic Sanskrit, and the verses are meant to be sung as sacred mantras. Many Hindu mantras honouring the different deities come from the Vedas. Some Vedic mantras are the Gayatri Mantra, Saraswati Vandana Mantra.

The Vedas are so old that no one knows when they were first composed. They are thought to have been transmitted orally for centuries before they were written down around 1500 BCE.

What is a bhajan?

Bhajan is a **prayer** in the form of a song used to express the love and devotion of the devotee. 'Bhajan' in Sanskrit means singing the name of the Lord. In general, a bhajan has simple, heartfelt words and an easy tune, encouraging the listeners also to sing.

Bhajan songs are sung often at religious gatherings to create a soulful atmosphere. Someone may start a bhajan and the listeners may join in. Bhajans have been popular since the medieval ages, and many saints and spiritual personalities have composed Bhajans. The Bhajans of Tulsidas, Meera Bai and Kabir are well loved by common people for their deep meaning and lilting tunes.

What is Aum?

Aum or Om is the short form or syllable of the word **"Omkara"** a Sanskrit sound which means 'that sounded out loudly'. Hindus believe Om is the most sacred sound from which all creation began. Some Hindus believe that it is the signature or the symbol of God.

This sacred sound was first mentioned in the Upanishads, which are the sacred texts of the Hindu religion. Since ancient times, saints, seers and sages have chanted the sound of "Aum" during meditation and worship. This is because the syllable is believed to invoke God's blessings.

Apart from being a basic sound, Om is also considered as an important symbol by both Hindus and Buddhists. The sound of Om is used often during yoga sessions and helps people breathe deeply and gain more concentration. You will find many Hindus chanting – "Hari Om Hare Krishna" in the morning.

What is the swastika?

The swastika is an **ancient Indian symbol** that goes back at least 30 centuries. It represents life, light good fortune and strength. This word comes from Sanskrit and contains the expression '**Su**' which means good.

The swastika shows a cross with all its arms of equal length. Each arm is bent at right angles in a clockwise direction. The Swastika is painted often with red vermillion on pots used during Hindu worship rituals. You will see the swastika sign on Hindu temples particularly at the entrances.

Much later during the World War 2, the Nazis reversed the original meaning of this symbol and it became a symbol of hated and became feared. The swastika when used in a positive sense is a sacred symbol and is seen as such in both Hinduism and Buddhism.

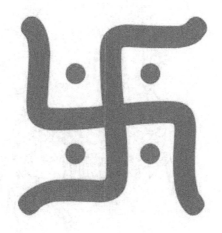

What is Ishvara?

Ishvara is how ancient Hinduism addresses the **supreme creator** or God. Hinduism is a polytheistic religion, which means this religion worships many Gods and Goddesses. In many of the mantras written in the holy books such as the Upanishads and the Manu Smriti, there is a reference to Ishvara.

Ishwara means 'lord' or 'master'. It is sometimes affixed after the names of various important deities. Therefore, one name for *Lord Shiva* is *Maheshwara* which means the Great God.

There are many variations in Hinduism and some believe in Ishvara and some don't. Just remember, Ishvara or Ishvar simply means God in Hinduism.

Who is a sadhu?

A sadhu refers to a Hindu **holy man or woman** (called sadhvi). The word 'sadhu' derives from 'sadhana', meaning concentrated, intense and long-term devotion to a higher being. Thus the sadhu is supposed to spend his time engaged in sadhana. This sadhana is aimed at reaching the supreme goal of moksha or liberation.

The sadhu detaches from his family and worldly comforts. Many sadhus wear saffron clothes, a color that represents detachment or renunciation. The lifestyle of a sadhu is that of a wanderer, going from place to place. He or she lives on alms often, and eats fruits or other foods found growing in nature.

Meaning of aarti in Hinduism?

Aarti or 'Arathi' is a basic ritual used in **'puja'** or the worship of Hindu Gods and Goddesses. In this ritual, a lamp is lit and a ceremony with the light is performed to express love and devotion for God.

Doing an aarti ceremony is an art in itself. The priest uses different movement patterns and styles of his hand and often chants mantras in praise of the idol. There may also be songs and hymns in praise of the deity. Aarti is usually performed at the end of a worship session.

The aarti dance in Durga Puja in Bengal and the daily aarti ceremony at the Dashashwamedh Ghat in Varanasi are delights to watch.

The blessing of the Gods and Goddesses can be taken through the aarti. It is thought they will bless the devotee through the flames of the aarti.

What is ahimsa?

The term 'ahimsa' basically means **non-violence** in thought, spoken words and action. In another sense, the term ahimsa also means practicing compassion and love for all loving creatures and avoiding injuring them in any way.

According to the ancient Hindu scriptures, ahimsa means true sacrifice, forgiveness, power and strength. In the epic Mahabharata, ahimsa or non-violence is regarded to be the highest moral virtue.

Hinduism holds that ahimsa is a path to lead a good life. It helps one to have a pure mind and soul.

This doctrine has been celebrated in Hinduism and particularly in Buddhism by Lord Buddha. In recent times, Mahatma Gandhi was one of the persons who followed and taught ahimsa.

Do Hindus eat meat?

Hindus are mainly known as vegetarians though some Hindus do eat meat. Generally in Hinduism, not eating meat is a way to maintain good health and happiness.

Hinduism also strongly believes in the cycle of **'karma'** or action. According to this belief, if a person causes harm or pain to any living creature, they will receive the same harm or injury in their turn in this life or the next.

The traditional food of the Hindus usually consists of different kinds of vegetables, fruits, rice, wheat, milk products, pulses, grains etc. In the modern world, Hindus are known for a varied and rich vegetarian cuisine with interesting dishes made of pulses, vegetables, and milk and soya products.

Many modern Hindus do eat meat, fish and eggs.

Why don't Hindus eat beef?

Hindus do not eat beef because in Hinduism, the cow is a symbol of wealth, health and abundance. The cow gives milk which is used in many religious rituals, sacrifices and the household.

The cow is associated with the Hindu god Krishna who was said to be a cowherd. At the same time, it must be kept in mind that beef eating was quite common during the ancient Vedic times in India, because it was once believed that only a Hindu who eats beef is a good Hindu. Gradually this changed as the cow came to be considered a sacred animal.

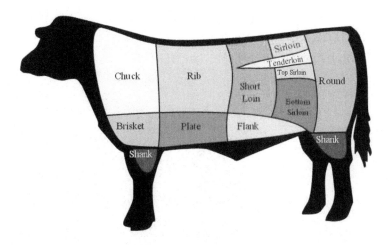

Do Hindus eat pork?

Eating pork has not been strongly prohibited in Hinduism. But at the same time, the religion would not entertain the eating of pork because it would lead to the killing of a living creature which is an act of violence and is looked down upon.

Another reason for not eating pork could be because of hygiene issues. The pig is often considered a dirty animal and therefore eating its meat is thought to be unhealthy.

Hindus who absolutely do not eat meat also do not eat pork while some Hindus who are meat-eaters may have pork occasionally.

There is no text in Hinduism that specifically forbids pork, however often Indian restaurants do not have pork on the menu.

Why is the River Ganges holy?

Hindus consider the River Ganges scared. They think of this river as their mother and even call it **mother Ganga**. Hindus from all over India and the world come to the river to bathe. Some of the places where the river is thought to be sacred are Varanasi, Allahabad, Gangotri and Haridwar. Hindus bathe in the River Ganges to wash away the sins and free themselves from the recycle birth.

It is thought that the River Ganges originated from Lord Shiva's hair to cater for India's demands which included water for humans and cattle and for use in growing crops.

Some people take water from the Ganges in bottles so that they can sprinkle some of the holy water in their homes and also use it during their pujas (worship). If you see Hindu priests sprinkling water around the temple, most likely it is water from the River Ganges. It is called "Ganja Jal" in Hindi.

The holy River Ganges

What is the importance of the lotus in Hinduism?

The lotus is a traditional symbol of **purity and beauty** in Hinduism. It is said that the lotus arose from the navel of Lord Vishnu. Beautiful eyes are often compared to lotus petals in the Hindu holy books.

A fully bloomed lotus is seen as a symbol of consciousness (complete awareness). The flower is used in the worship of many Hindu deities. The worship of Durga in Eastern India is done with 108 lotus flowers. Goddess Lakshmi is described as sitting on a white lotus.

In yoga, the ancient wellness practice too, the lotus is mentioned. Padmasana is a famous aasana or yoga posture which is inspired by the graceful form of a lotus. The lotus is also a sacred flower in Buddhism.

Why do Hindu women put a dot on their head?

Hindu women put a dot (called the **bindi**) usually of red colour in the centre of the forehead. A bindi can also be of other colours. Generally a dot or a bindi is regarded to be the symbol of being a Hindu woman.

Putting a dot on the forehead has another importance. In Hinduism, the mid-point of the forehead between the eyebrows is supposed to be the zone of wisdom. So the bindi is believed to restore concentration of the mind.

The bindi is also believed to protect against bad luck or demons. It is also put by Hindu women on the forehead as a beauty mark during festivals or rituals such as the wedding ceremony, Holi and so on. A married Hindu woman is expected to put a bindi along with vermillion on their forehead.

Why do Hindus put a dot on their forehead?

Hindus often wear a dot-like mark called the **'tilak'** on their forehead especially during religious ceremonies. The custom of wearing 'tilak' goes back many centuries.

The tilak can be of different colours and shapes, and stands for different things. In some cases, it shows which God the person worships. People who worship Vishnu and those who worship Shiva, for example, have different marks on their forehead.

The tilak is also a symbol of purity, and often it is worn during 'puja' or worship of a deity. Many Hindus would have a very faint tilak on their forehead and you won't be able to tell if that person is wearing the tilak or not.

Hindus in the olden days were strict followers of the caste system in which people belonged to different 'varnas or castes' according to their occupation. The four varnas had different markings to distinguish them from each other. But this is not the case anymore.

Wearing the tilak and bindi on the forehead

Who is Lord Ganesha?

Ganesha is an important God worshipped by Hindus. His worship is associated with new beginnings, prosperity and success. He is supposed to have written the Ramayana, the ancient Hindu epic. Ganesha is traditionally worshipped with an elephant head and the body of a man.

He is jovial, has a big belly, and is fond of eating sweets. That is why you will find him holding a sweet in his hand. According to the ancient Hindu texts, Ganesha is the child of Lord Shiva and Parvati. Lots of interesting stories have been told about him and his vehicle the tiny mouse.

Ganesha is also called by different names such as Ekdanta, Ganapati, Siddhi Vinayaka etc. In total, he has 108 names. In Maharashtra, Ganesha Chaturthi is an important festival, celebrating the birth of Lord Ganesha.

How did Ganesha get the elephant head?

One day Parvati got muddied and wanted to take a bath. She retreated in private, cleaned off the dirt and with it, created a small child Ganesha. She instructed Ganesha to stand guard and not let anybody come and disturb her privacy.

Shiva her husband came by and Ganesha not recognizing him stopped him. Furiously Shiva chopped off the little one's head. When Parvati told him the story of how Ganesha was their son, Shiva realised what he had done. He fixed an elephant head, the sign of immense wisdom, onto the body of the little boy. Thus Ganesha got his elephant head.

Who is Lord Rama?

Lord Rama is the chief character of the Indian epic Ramayana after which the epic is named. He is the son of King Dasharatha of the kingdom of Ayodha. His wife is named Sita.

He went away on exile to the forest to honor the word of his father. There, he had many adventures and in one of them, Sita was captured by Ravana, the king of Lanka. Rama waged a fight to win back Sita and avenge her for being taken away by force.

Lord Rama is supposed to be an avatar or incarnation of Lord Vishnu in a human form (find out more about Vishnu below). His name is considered sacred by Hindus. Many Hindus chant the name of Rama by saying 'Hare Rama'. In the picture below, Rama is seen in the middle, Sita on his left and his brother Laksmana on his right.

Lord Rama with Laksmana and Sita

Who is Lord Shiva?

Lord Shiva is part of the holy Hindu trinity in which the other two gods are Brahma and Vishnu. Brahma is the Creator, Vishnu is the Preserver and Shiva is the supreme destroyer. He is supposed to destroy evil.

The most unworldly of the gods, Shiva wears rags and has ashes smeared on his body. He lives high in the Himalayas with his wife Parvati. Shiva is known for his detachment from the world. When furious, Shiva is said to dance the Tandava, the dance of destruction. In this form he is called the Nataraja.

There are many Shiva temples in India. Those who worship Shiva exclusively are called Shaivites. Shaivites consider Lord Shiva as the Supreme Being. They consider him as the one who created, the one who preserves and the one who will destroy – the complete God.

Who is Lord Krishna?

Lord Krishna is the incarnation of Lord Vishnu, the preserver. He came to earth to restore virtue and righteousness to the world. (Find out who is Vishnu below).

Lord Krishna grew up as a cowherd in Vrindavan, being playful with beautiful maidens, and his beloved Radha. He is depicted often with a beautiful flute, playing with the maidens in the pastures. He had many adventures from his early childhood some of which included defeating the demons called Kaliya, Putana, etc.

His story is told in the Mahabharata, the vast epic about the battle between the Pandavas and the forces of evil, the Kauravas. Lord Krishna sided with the Pandavas and gave the Pandava prince, Arjuna advice about the world. This advice became the Bhagavad Gita, a holy book of Hindu philosophy.

Radha and Krishna

Who is Lord Vishnu?

Lord Vishnu is the Supreme Preserver, while Shiva is the Destroyer and Brahma the Creator in the holy Hindu trinity. Vishnu sustains all of creation and everything in it, according to Hindu philosophy. His consort is Lakshmi. He is supposed to uphold dharma, justice and peace.

There are nine incarnations of Vishnu which show how powerful he is. He came to the earth in different forms including those of animals. Some important incarnations of Vishnu are the Kurma avatar (tortoise), the Meen avatar (fish) and the Vamana avatar (dwarf). His other avatars include Lord Rama and Krishna which you read about earlier.

Vishnu is also called by two other names, Narayana and Hari. Those who worship Vishnu exclusively are known as Vaishnavites.

Who is Goddess Durga?

Durga is the universal Mother Goddess, known for her supreme power, compassion and majesty. She is mentioned in several of the Vedas.

Durga is believed to be a vanquisher of all evil in the world. She is also known as Parvati, the wife of Shiva (Lord Ganesh's mother). Her other form in which she is worshipped is Kali, Santoshi, Chamunda and Kundalini.

There are many stories about this powerful Goddess. In one story; she is armed, has three eyes, ten hands and rides a lion as she kills the demon Mahishasura. This victory of good over evil is celebrated in the grand Durga Puja, which takes place in India mainly in Eastern India and Mysore in South India.

Who is Goddess Lakshmi?

Goddess Lakshmi is the giver of peace, beauty, prosperity and wealth. She is shown seated on a fully bloomed lotus. The lotus on which she sits is the symbol of grace and beauty.

She is worshipped in Hindu homes in many parts of India. She rides an elegant white swan which floats on the water. She is sometimes shown to be holding a sheaf of rice grains in her hand. Goddess Lakshmi is the consort of Vishnu. Since she is the bringer of wealth, she is also worshipped by business people. Lakshmi Puja is celebrated on a full moon night.

Who is the Monkey God?

The Monkey God is Lord Hanuman, whose story is told in the Ramayana. Hanuman, Rama's chief ally, rallied many monkey soldiers to build a bridge of stones and rocks across the sea so that Rama could reach Lanka and rescue Sita.

Hanuman is famous for his courage, loyalty and devotion to Lord Rama. He is supposed to be the son of Pavana, the Wind God. In the Ramayana, he flies with a mountain in one hand, crosses the sea in one giant leap, sets fire with one sweep of his tail to Lanka along with many other brave acts.

The "**Hanuman Chalisa**" is a set of hymns (or mantras) in praise of Hanuman and many Hindu children learn it by heart. It is said that those who chant the "Hanuman Chalisa" everyday become free from disease and evil influences. Each verse of the Hanuman Chalisa has its own significance.

What is Holi?

Holi is the ancient Hindu festival of colors. It occurs on a full moon night at the beginning of spring. Holi is traditionally believed to be the time when Lord Krishna played with colors with the beautiful maidens and his beloved Radha in Vrindavan.

The festival of Holi is named after Holika, a she-demon who was vanquished by Lord Rama. So a straw effigy representing Holika is burnt on the night before Holi. On the day of Holi people; young and old, smear each other with colored powders and spray colored water. The celebrations take place both inside the homes and out on the streets. It's a national holiday all over India. Holi is a lot of fun!

What is Diwali?

Diwali is also known as Deepavali. It celebrates Lord Rama's return to Ayodhya with his wife Sita and brother Lakshmana after his exile. The people of Ayodhya lit lamps to celebrate the safe return of their beloved prince. The festivities also celebrate the defeat of evil and the victory of goodness.

The Diwali festival takes place every autumn. People light up candles and clay lamps in the evening. People also burst different kinds of crackers and eat sweets. Lakhsmi (the Goddess of wealth) and Ganesha Puja (worship) are also a part of celebrating Diwali in Northern India. Diwali is a national holiday for all Indians.

What is Raksha Bandhan?

Raksha Bandhan celebrates the bonding of a brother with his sister. In Hindi, 'Raksha' means protection, and 'Bandhan' means bond.

Raksha Bandhan is supposed to have begun in ancient times in Rajasthan when the soldiers used to go to war. Before their departure, the sisters prayed for their brother's safe return and tied a thread called 'rakhi' on their brother's wrist. Sisters also tie the rakhi (like the one below) on their brother's wrist as a symbol of love and in return brothers promises to take care of their sisters and protect her. There are many types of rakhi available in the market even Harry Potter ones.

This festival is celebrated in many parts of India. On the day of the festival, the sister decorates the brother's forehead with a tilak or dot made of colored grains, rice etc. Gifts are also exchanged between the siblings. This festival usually occurs on a full moon day in autumn.

What is the caste system?

The ancient Hindu social order consisted of four **varnas** (castes) or divisions according to job role and responsibility. They are Kshatriya (warriors) Brahmana (who carried out sacred rites), Vaishya (traders), and Shudras (who performed cleaning services to keep society running smoothly). The Brahmanas were naturally the highest born (upper caste) and the Kshatriyas were the noblest. The Vaishyas were next in the social order, and the Shudras were the lowest (lower caste).

In the beginning, the varnas were given to people according their jobs. Gradually, the varnas grew into a strict caste system. In this system, the Brahmanas made up strict rules for other to follow. It even prevented marriages between the castes.

Modern Indians like Mahatma Gandhi and others raised their voice against this system. In many places in India, the caste system is still responsible for grave injustices against the lower castes. Caste discrimination is not banned in India.

What is reincarnation?

Reincarnation is an important concept in Hinduism. It is based on the belief that the **soul is eternal** (do not die) while the body can change.

According to the ancient Hindu belief, people have many lives and are born many times. In some births, they may be born in forms other than human beings. So, someone who is a human in this life may be reborn as an elephant or an insect, in another birth. The Law of Karma, which is the law of right action, governs the form in which a person is born. This means that you are reborn according to the life you live and the things you do. If you are a bad person then you might become an insect in the next life and if you do good things then you might lead a very nice life in the next. This will carry on till you become the perfect person and you will be rewarded by becoming free from reincarnation (called Moksha). You will no longer be reborn, you are free and become part of God himself.

Since Buddhism developed out of Hinduism, the idea of reincarnation is also present in Buddhism along with Jainism. There are similar beliefs in Sikhism too.

The soul remains but body changes

What is moksha?

Moksha is the supreme release from the cycle of lives and deaths. In Hindu belief, the soul is born in different bodily forms in different births. The soul is born on earth as many times as it is needed to complete one's karma or action on earth.

When people do not need to be born any more, they attain Moksha, the supreme state of liberation. This is the state when you are free from the recycle of birth. Saints and holy men and women since ancient times have meditated, worshipped and performed many noble tasks in order to attain Moksha, considered the state of completion and perfection. The same belief in liberation is called **'Nirvana'** by Buddhists.

What is yoga?

Yoga in Sanskrit means **'fusion'**. It goes back to ancient Hindu belief in the integration of body, mind and soul. Yoga uses a combination of postures and breathing exercises to put the body into states of calm.

It used to be practiced by sages and holy people since the ancient times in India for meditation. Yoga keeps the body fit, the mind active and is known today for its many health benefits. Different postures of yoga are supposed to give benefits to different parts of the body, like the stomach, the waist, or the limbs.

Today, yoga is practiced the world over by people; young and old especially by those who want the health benefits of this ancient Indian wellness practice.

What is the Bhagavad Gita?

The Bhagavad Gita is one of the holy books of the Hindus. It gives advice about how to live life meaningfully. The name literally means the **'Song of God'** (Bhagavad is God and Gita is song). It is an account of the conversation of Arjuna, the Pandava prince had with Lord Krishna.

In the Mahabharata, the Pandavas were the forces of good, and they were fighting against their relatives, the Kauravas on the battlefield of Kurukshetra. When Arjuna refused to fight, Lord Krishna who was the charioteer of Arjuna's chariot, spoke. He spoke about the necessity of right action right now without worrying about what the fruit will be. He said, do the right actions and God will take care of the fruits of your actions.

What is the Ramayana?

The Ramayana is the oldest Indian epic. It is written in Sanskrit. The name 'Ramayana' means the story of Lord Rama. It is said to have been written by the great saint Valmiki between 500 and 100 BCE.

Lord Rama who was the prince of Ayodhya and the successor to the throne was sent to 14 years of exile by his father King Dasharatha. Rama's wife Sita too went with him to the jungle to spend the years of exile. Hanuman, Ravana and many other characters feature in the story. When Rama returned from his exile, the people of Ayodhya celebrated Diwali in his honour.

The tale of Ramayana is all about bravery, loyalty, devotion and wisdom. It is still narrated and sung in many parts of India.

What is the Mahabharata?

The Mahabharata is the largest epic in the world. It runs over 110 thousand couplets (lines of rhymes) in Sanskrit. The name of the epic means Great Bharata or India.

This epic is the world's longest poem that has a wide variety of characters, events and a very complicated storyline about a great battle. Its deeper discussions are about ethics, morality, virtue, politics, royalty and a lot of other things.

The core of the Mahabharata is said to be dictated by Lord Ganesha. The other parts were added by the saint Ved Vyasa.

What is aatma?

Aatma or Aatman is soul in Sanskrit. It is also called the Jeeva-aatma, meaning soul of a being. According to Hinduism, the aatman is eternal and never dies. It is separate from the body. So, even after a person dies, the aatma remains. Nothing can destroy it. It occupies many different bodies in many life times.

The aatma is the pure and sacred seat of God. It is completely spiritual in nature. When the aatma completes its task or karma (deed) on earth over as many lifetimes as it takes, it reaches the supreme state of moksha or liberation from the cycle of life and death. After attaining moksha, the aatma of a person merges with the Paramatma, the great creator.

What is maya?

Maya is a philosophical concept discussed in the Bhagavad Gita. The word occurs in the sacred book four times. Maya is the Sanskrit word for **'illusion'**.

According to Hindu belief, the world as we see it is an illusion. Just because we see things a certain way, does not mean it is the real thing. The truth lies beyond the physical reality veiled by maya. Till we remove this veil, we cannot see the reality and the deeper truth. Many of our strong feelings and emotions contribute to maya. All our actions are guided by maya. Detachment and separation is needed in order to see the world beyond appearance.

What is the Gayatri Mantra?

The Gayatri Mantra is a sacred composition that many Hindus chant. This mantra is a part of the Rig Veda, one of the four important Vedas of the ancient times.

The Gayatri Mantra is a Sanskrit verse and is said to have been composed by the saint Viswamitra. It is written in a metre (a verse of the Vedas) called 'Gayatri' during the Vedic times, which is how it gets its name. The Gayatri Mantra is dedicated to Savitri, a name for the sun who is the giver of life. It is usually chanted at sunrise or sunset.

In the olden days, only Brahmin males could recite this mantra. Now, any Hindu can chant this sacred verse.

What is the Saraswati Mantra?

The Saraswati Mantra is dedicated to Saraswati, the Hindu Goddess of wisdom, knowledge and arts. This mantra is also called the Saraswati Vandana where Vandana means song of worship.

This Sanskrit verse praises the many splendors of Saraswati. In this mantra, Saraswati is described to be seated on a white fully bloomed lotus. She holds a beautiful stringed musical instrument called the veena in one hand. She is white like the moon and is dressed all in white, the color of purity.

This mantra is very popular among students, teachers and musicians. Reciting the Saraswati Mantra is supposed to bring the blessings of this Goddess for artistic works and studies.

What are the other Hindu Festivals?

Hindus celebrate many festivals all year round. At the start of the year in January is Maha Sankranti, a harvest festival. In the spring time, festival of Vasant Panchami celebrates the worship of Saraswati. Around April, the festival of Rama Navami celebrates the birth of Rama.

The monsoons are the time for Ratha Yatras. In Eastern India at a place called Puri, grand chariots are paraded with the idols of deities Jagannath, Balaram and Subhadra seated on them. Janmashtami is another festival during the monsoons where Hindus celebrate the birth of Lord Krishna.

Then comes a festival called Ganesh Chaturthi, a grand celebration dedicated to Lord Ganesha. In autumn, the festival of Navaratri is celebrated over nine days and nights, ending with Dussehra.

Dhanteras is another festival which is about welcoming wealth and prosperity into the home usually celebrated a day before Diwali.

In addition, various regions of India have their local festivals, such as Onam, Pongal, Vaishakhi and many others.

Lord Ganesha

What is Namaste?

Namaste is a Hindi word meaning 'salutation to you'. It also means, 'I bow to the goodness in you'. It is derived from the Sanskrit word, 'Namaskar'.

The Namaste is a gesture with the hands that is made to convey greetings. The hands are joined, palm to palm with the fingers pointing straight up, and the speaker may say 'Namaste'. The person to whom 'Namaste' is being said may also respond with a 'Namaste'. People also say 'Namaste' when they leave.

Sometimes, only the gesture is made without saying Namaste. The basic gesture is ancient and is used in many parts of Asia.

Where do Hindus go for pilgrimage?

Hindus since the ancient times have been going on pilgrimages in various parts of India. A pilgrimage is called 'Teerth'. Some of the most ancient places for pilgrimage are Badrinath, Kedarnath, Yamunotri and Gangotri in the Himalayas. These are popularly known together as the 'Char Dham' for Hindu pilgrims.

The Kumbh Mela held in Allahabad is one of the most famous locations for Hindu pilgrimage. Many foreigners also go there. Other popular pilgrimage sites in North India are Haridwar and Benares. Famous places in South India are Tirupati and Madurai. The Jagannath Temple in Puri and Vaishno Devi Temple in Jammu are also famous.

Why are cows sacred in Hinduism?

In the Rig Veda, the cow has been mentioned as a Goddess and is considered as a mother by Hindus. It provides milk which is the symbol of nurture, love and compassion. Since it gives milk which children drink to grow up - the cow has become a symbol of a mother.

It is a sin to harm the cow. This is why there are many cows often wandering near temples and holy places.

In ancient Hindu belief, Lord Krishna was a cow herder in Vrindavan. Since cows are associated with Lord Krishna, they are also considered scared. Traditionally, Hindus avoid eating cow meat.

Is Buddhism the same as Hinduism?

Buddhism grew out of Hinduism but it is a different and much younger religion compared to Hinduism. Buddhism is about the teachings of Gautama Buddha, who attained salvation and wanted to transmit the teachings to others.

The followers of Buddha compiled his teachings. Initially, Buddhism did not have idols. But later there were some Buddhist sects that welcomed idols of Lord Buddha and housed them in their monasteries. A belief in peace and non-violence is common to both the religions. Like Hindus, Buddhists too believe in the soul, the world as illusion, and liberation.

A difference between the two religions is that priests are not necessary in Buddhism and there is no caste system. Lord Buddha remained silent on the existence of God while we know that in Hinduism there are many Gods. In Hinduism, we know that once the soul is free from the recycle of birth, it comes part of God but what happens to the soul according to Buddhism is not clear that requires deep understanding on Buddhist philosophy.

Lord Buddha at the Bodi Temple

Who are the Jains?

The Jains belong to an ancient Indian religion called Jainism. The word 'Jain' comes from 'Jina', a Sanskrit word which means 'to conquer'.

The Jains believe in the teachings of their twenty four Tirthankaras, who are the Jain holy leaders. The Tirthankaras are supposed to have come in different ages. Adinatha is the first Tirthankara and the final Tirthankara is Mahavira.

Jainism is very strict about self-discipline and non-violence towards all creatures. This is why all Jains follow a completely vegetarian diet. Jains also have a strong tendency to be ascetics. The two main sections of Jainism are Svetambara and Digambara.

Many of the belief systems in Jainism are like Hinduism. However, they believe that Vedas have been corrupted over the years. Many Jains go to Hindu temples and celebrate Hindu festivals and consider themselves as part of the Hindu culture. But it is considered a different religion.

Jain Temple in Pawapuri, Bihar, India

Who are the Sikhs?

The Sikhs belong to the Sikh religion called Sikhism. Most of the Sikhs are from the state of Punjab in North India. The Sikh religion began to develop in the 15th century in the Northern part of India. The main proponent of this religion was Guru Nanak. 'Guru' is a Sanskrit word meaning 'teacher' or 'mentor'. In order to be a Sikh, one must believe in the five physical K's or symbols. They are; Kesh (uncut hair), Kara (steel bracelet), Kanga (wooden comb), Kaccha (cotton underwear) and Kirpan (sword).

The word 'Sikh' refers to being a learner or student. Other than Guru Nanak, the Sikh religion had many other gurus. The last and the tenth Guru was Guru Govind Singh.

The Sikhs believe in one God, and they worship in a temple called the Gurudwara, meaning the door of the Guru. Their holy book is the Guru Granth Sahib which is a collection of Sikh Guru's writings.

Sikh gurdwara at Patna Sahib

Message from the author

Thank you for buying this book. I hope you have learnt some good things about Hinduism. If you liked this book, then kindly consider leaving a feedback on the book's Amazon page. Also let your friends know about the book so that they too can learn about Hinduism.

If you have any questions on Hinduism then do feel free to send me a message or ask me a question. Feel free to visit my website for further information: http://www.shalusharma.com. If you want to learn more about India then you can subscribe to my newsletter on my website ShaluSharma.com.

Some of my other books include:

India For Kids: Amazing Facts About India
Essential Hindi Words And Phrases For Travelers To India
Life and Works of Aryabhata

Thank you and Namaste...PEACE TO ALL...

OM

Other titles by the author:

Made in the USA
Middletown, DE
19 July 2020